RETIREMENT
COLORING BOOK

THIS BOOK BELONGS TO

_____

First Printing, 2019

"There's never enough time to do all the nothing you want."

Bill Waterson, Calvin & Hobbes

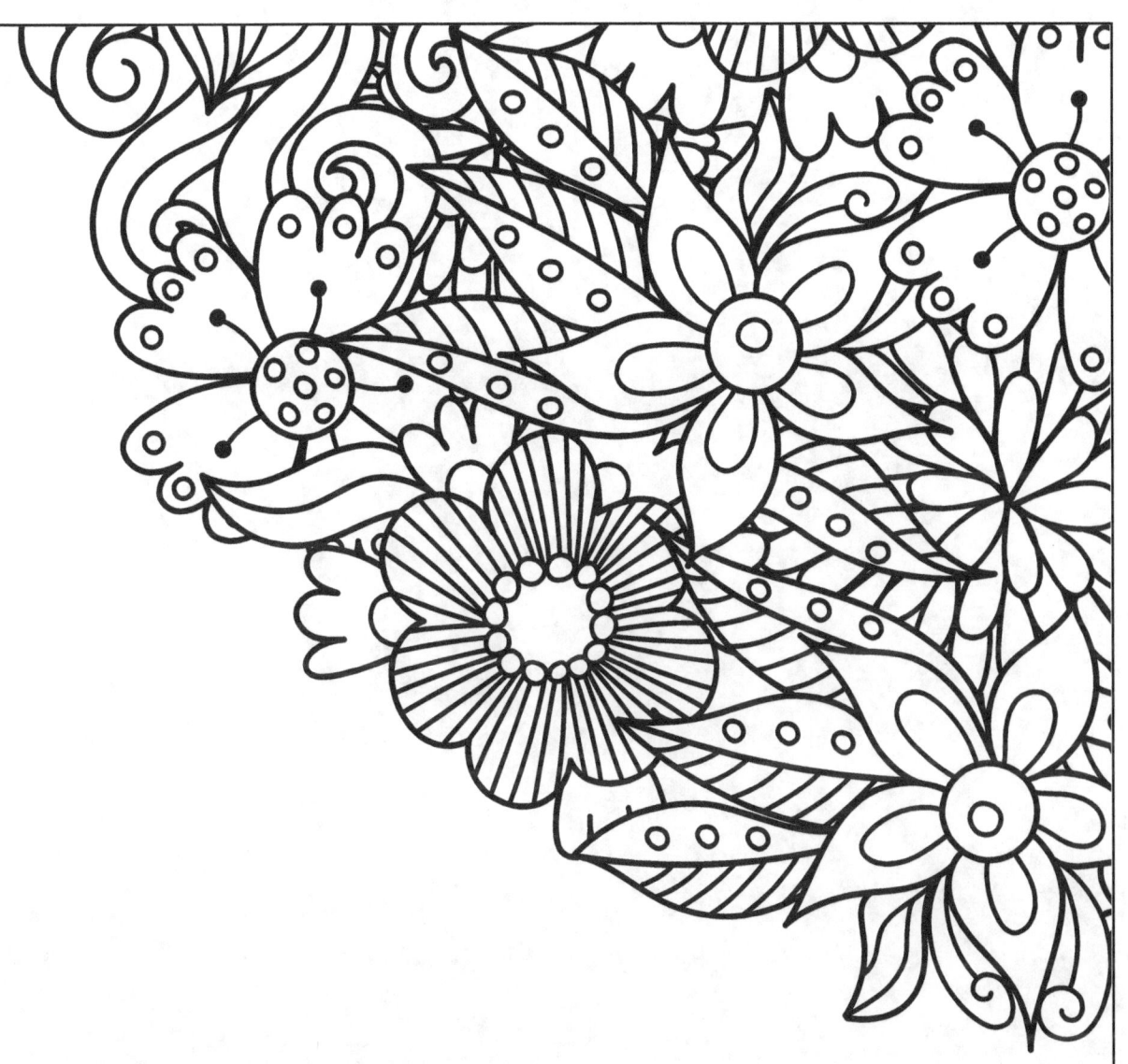

i'm retired
you are not

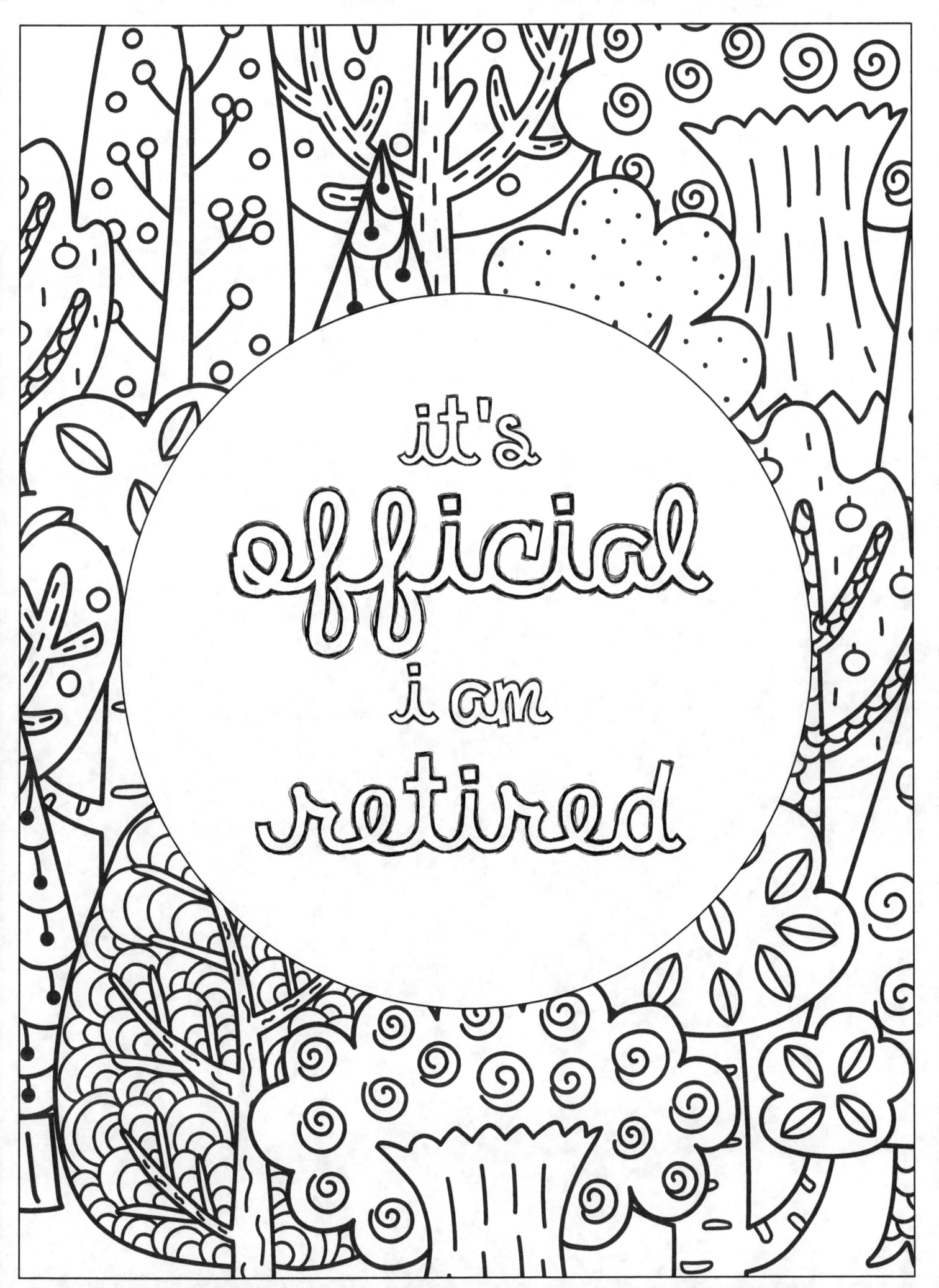

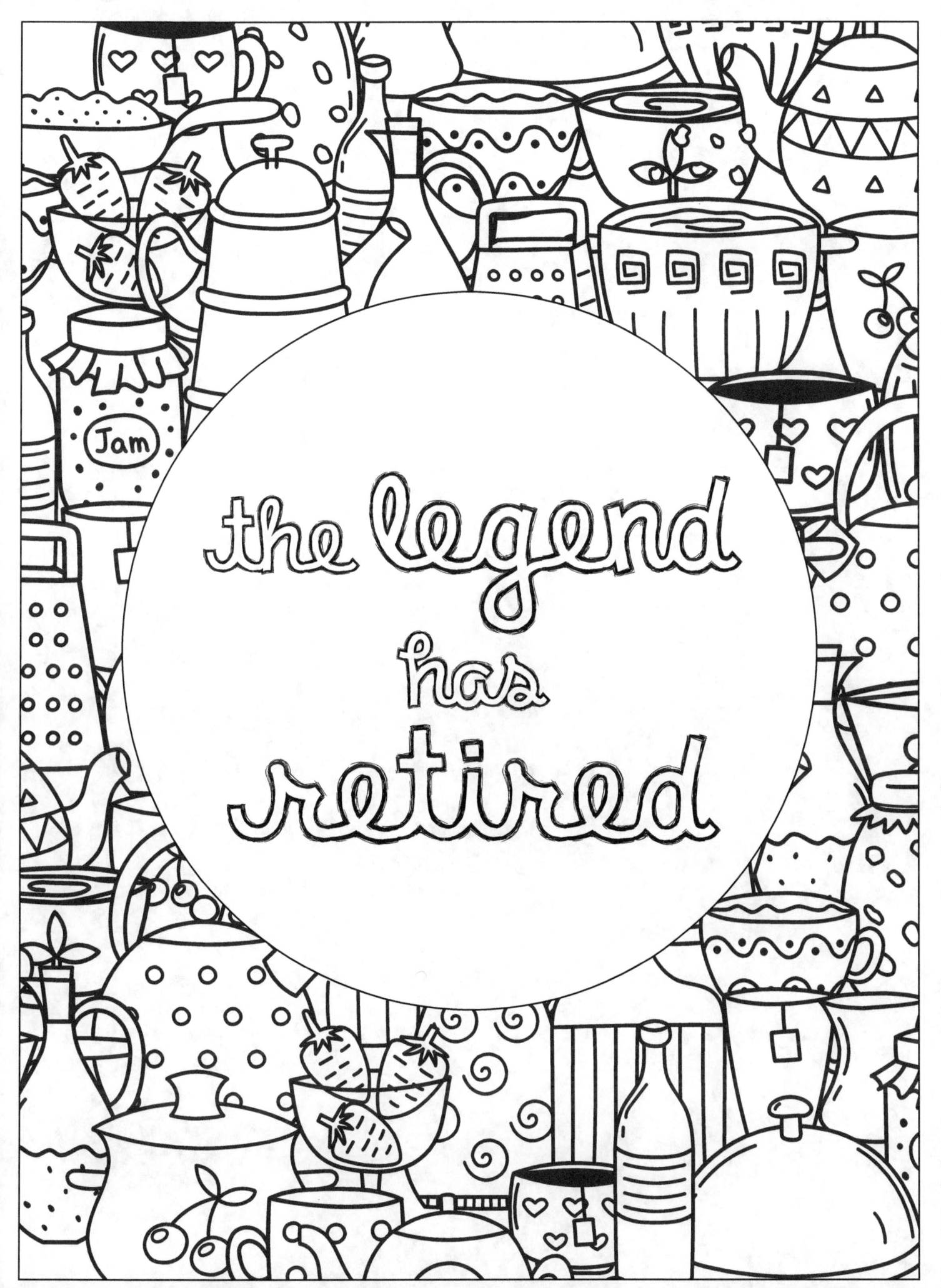

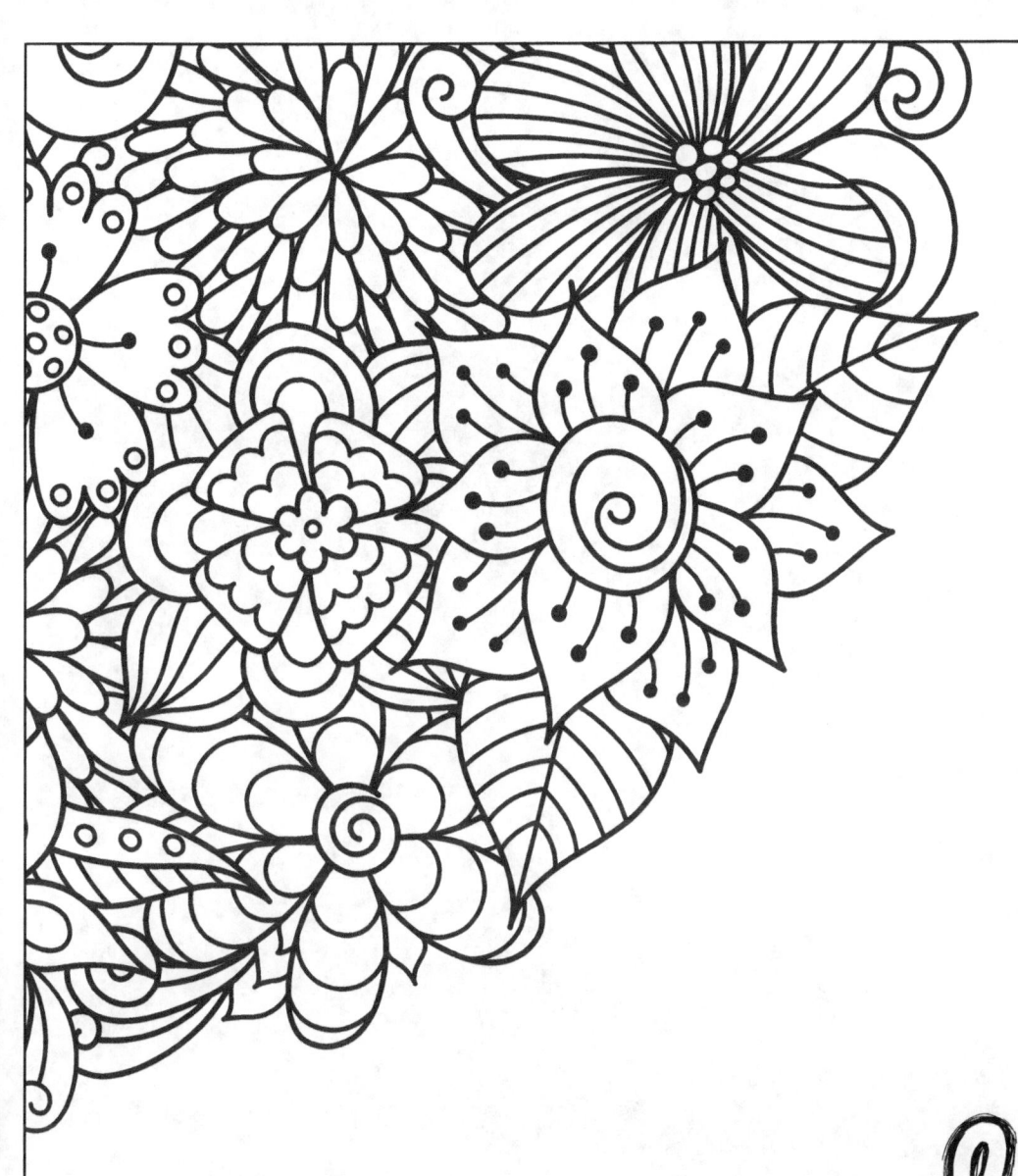

doing what
i want when
i want

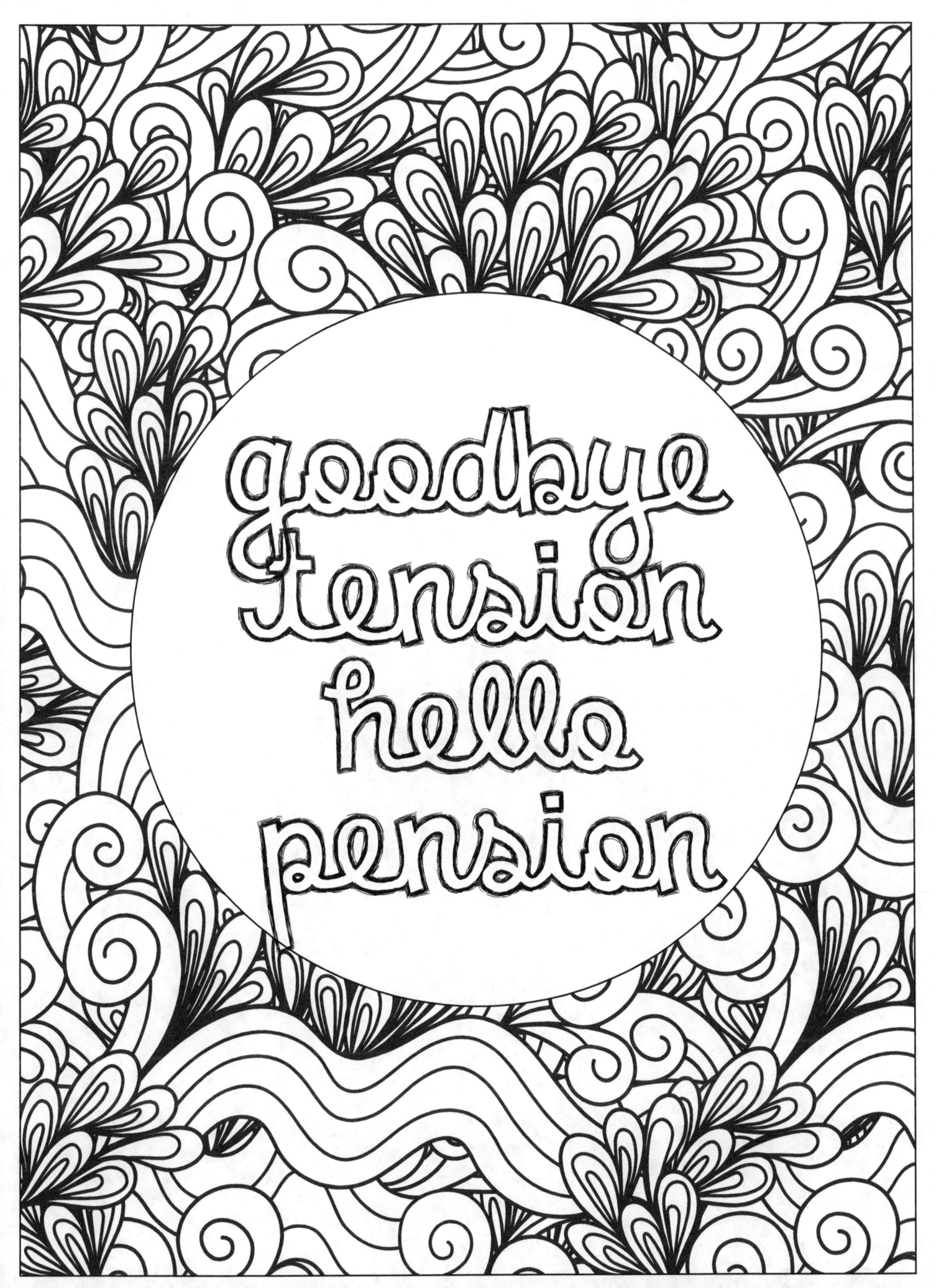

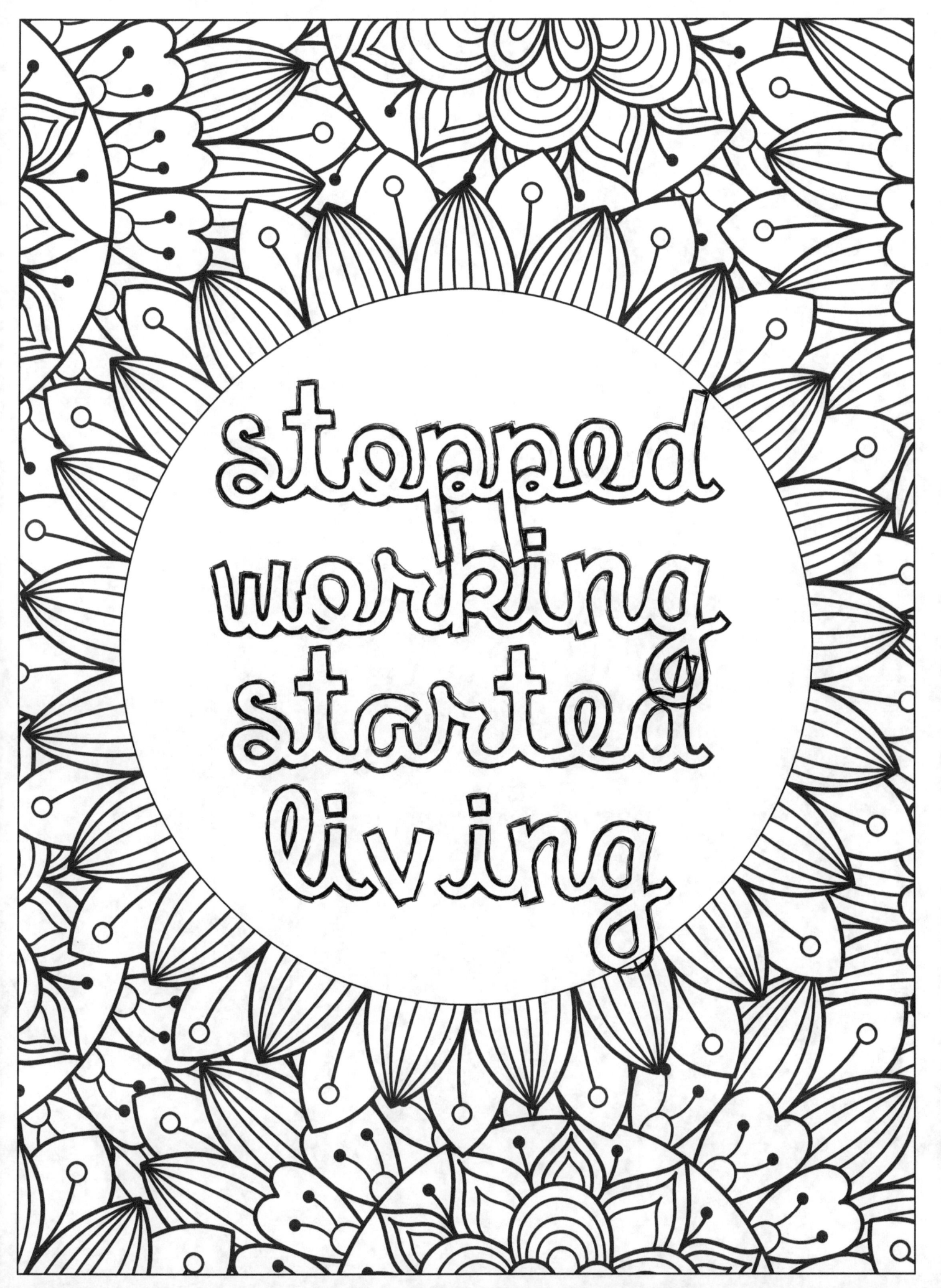

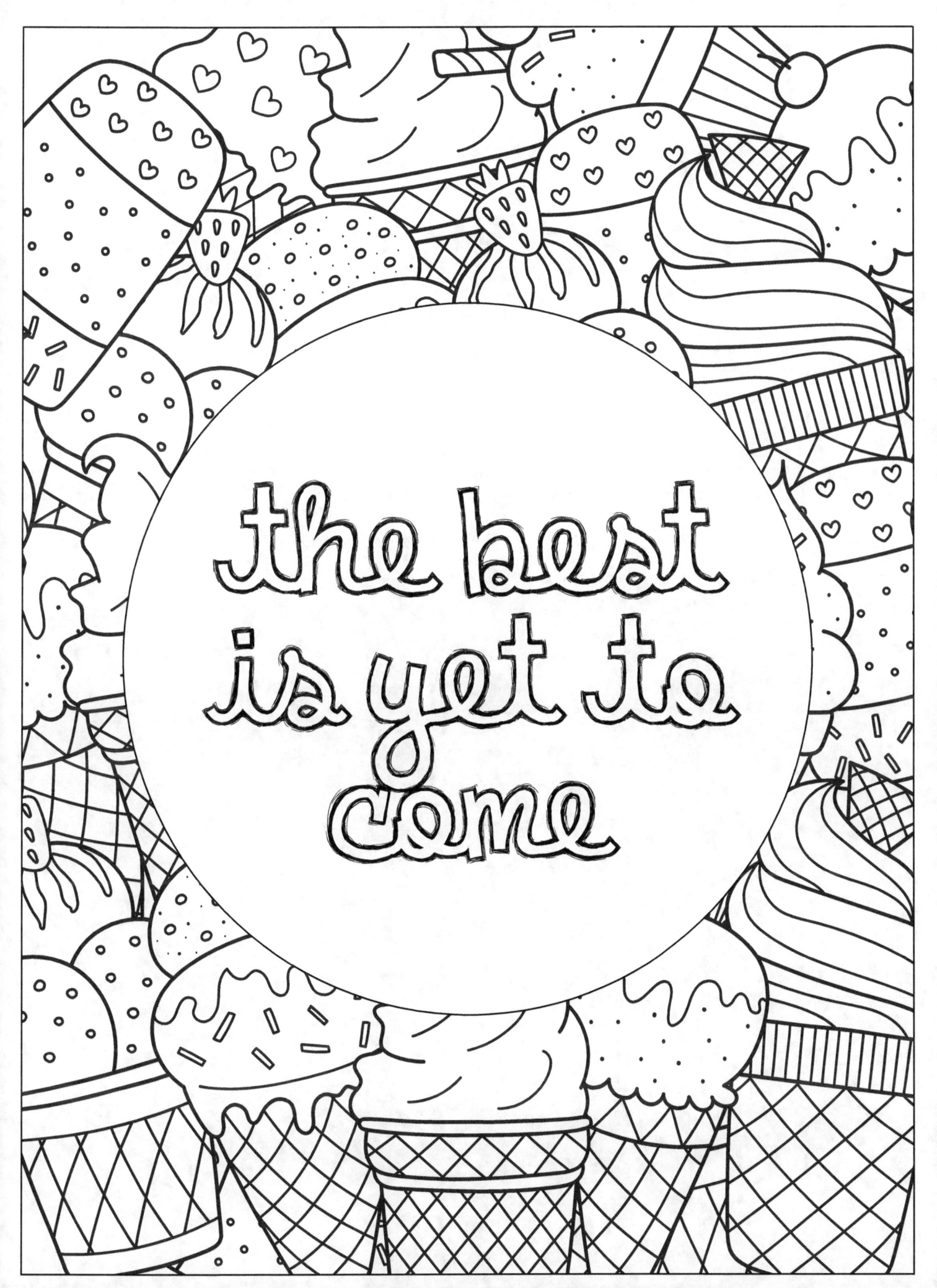

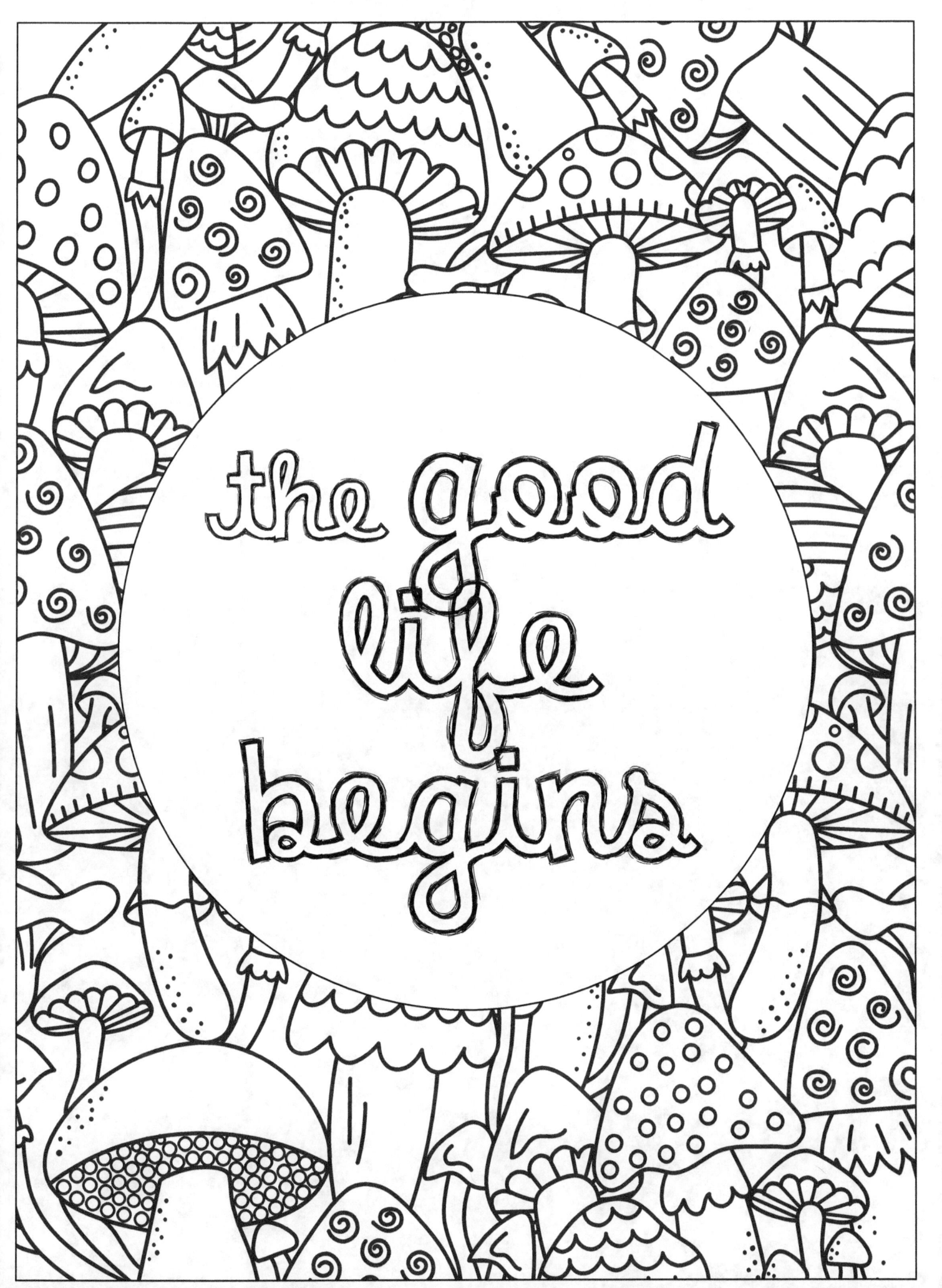

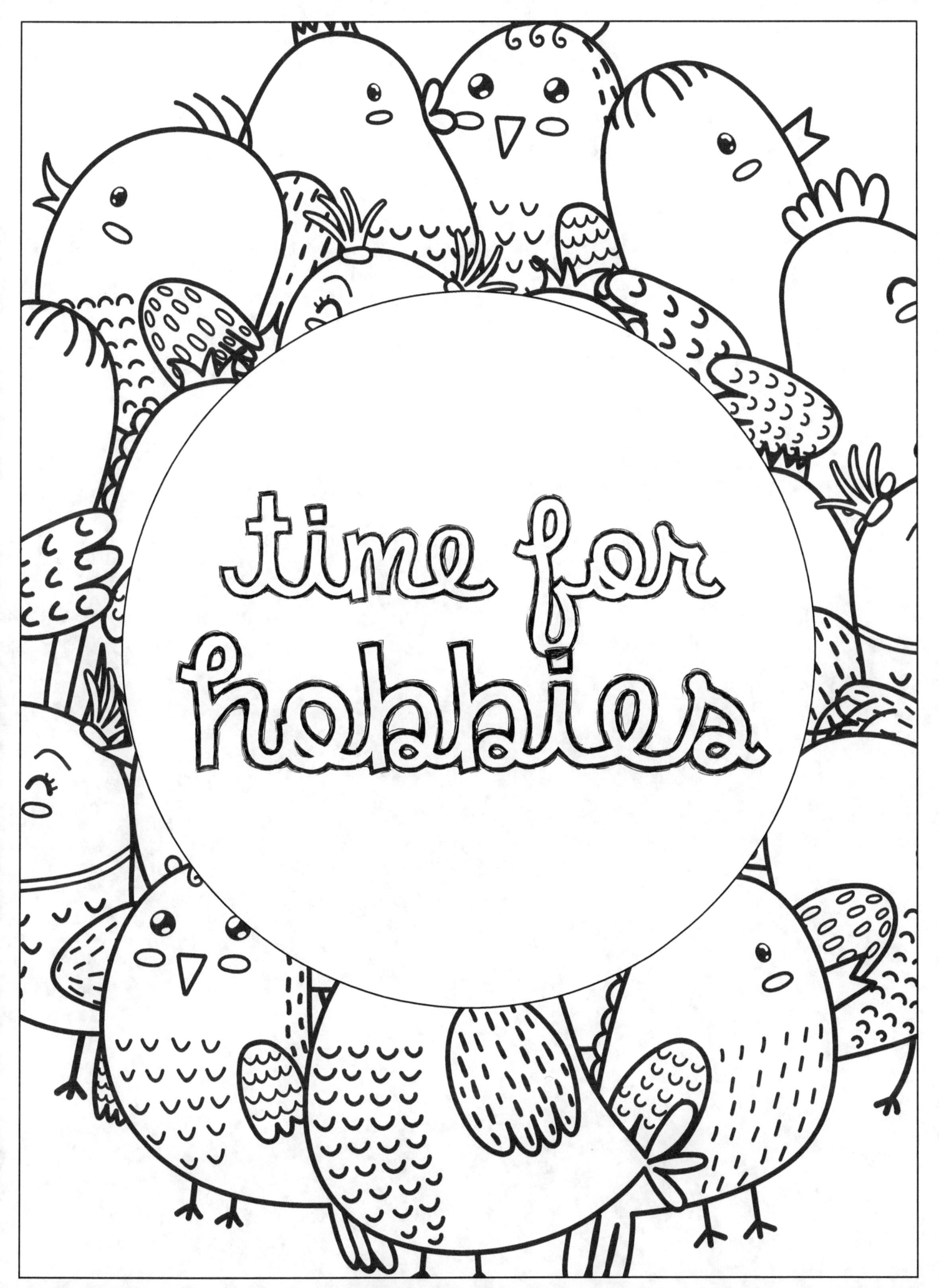

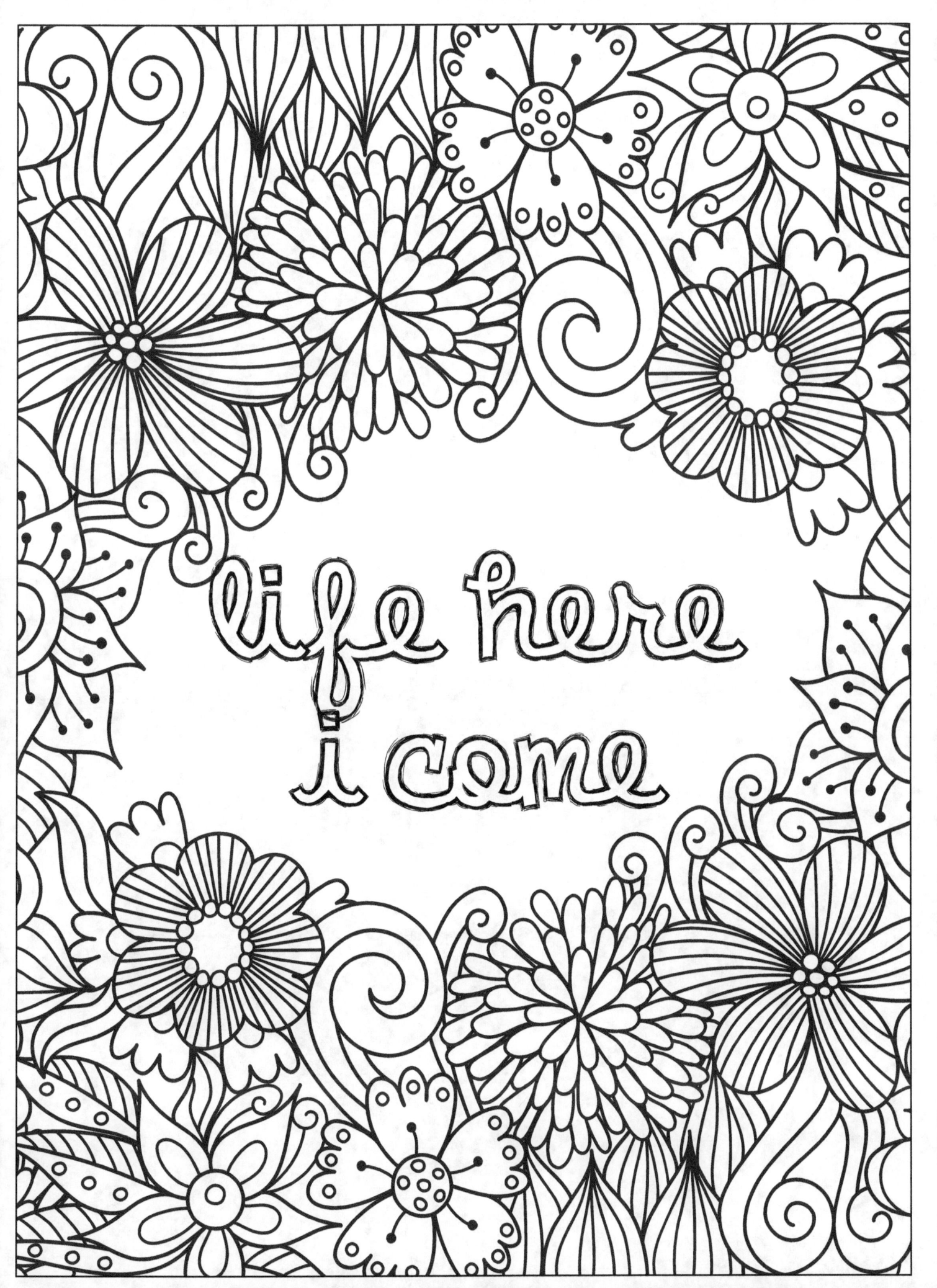

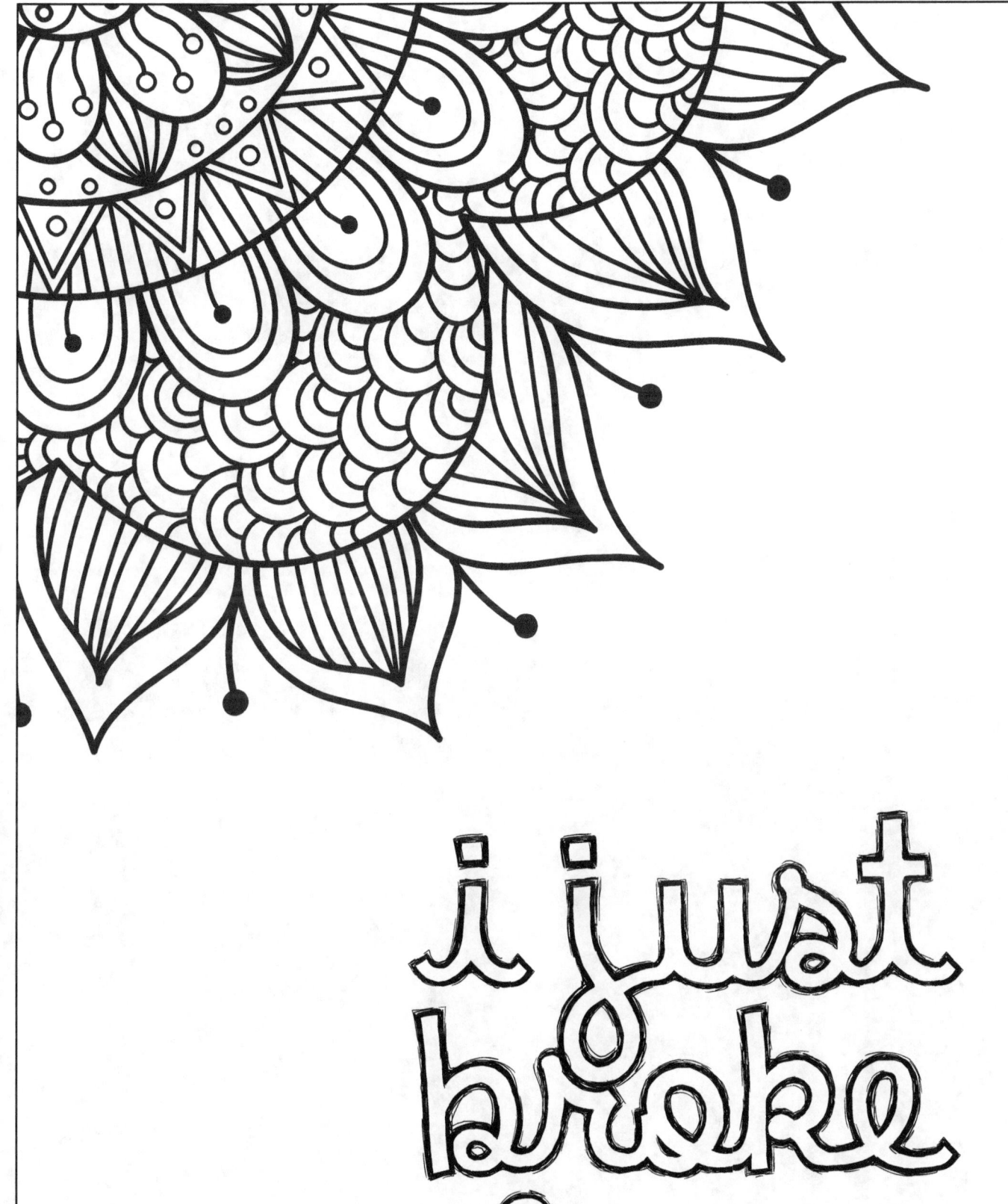

i just broke free

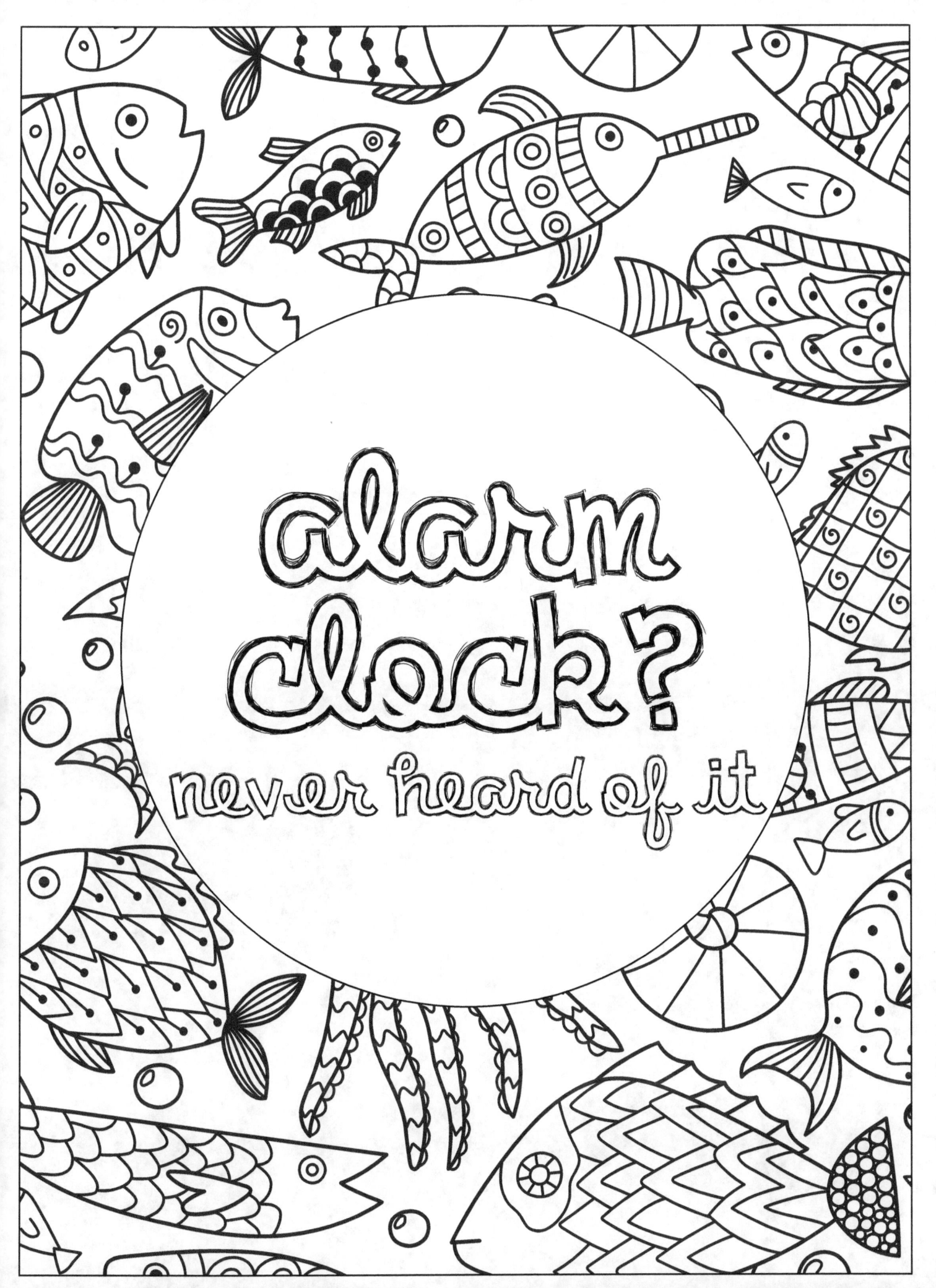

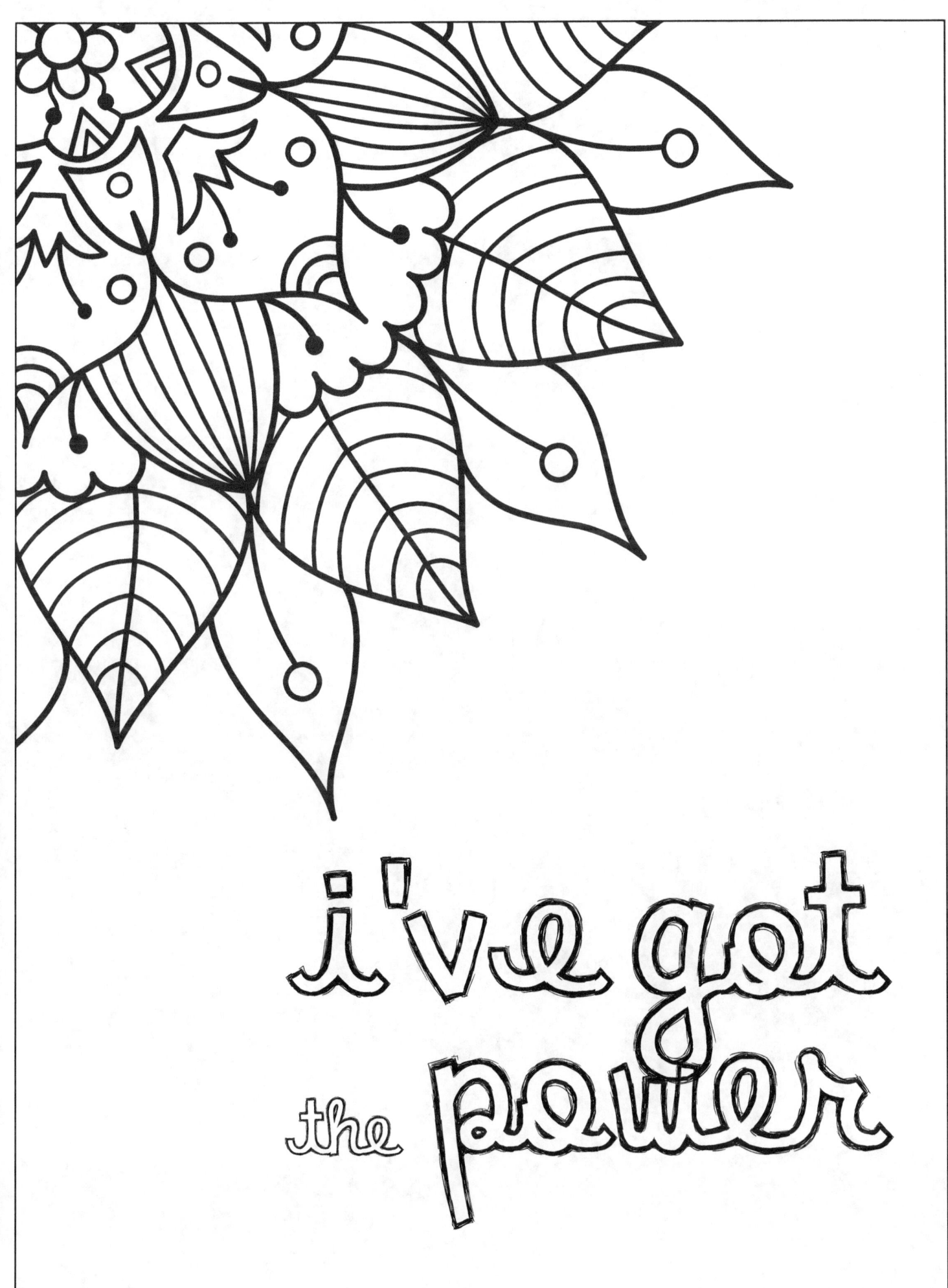

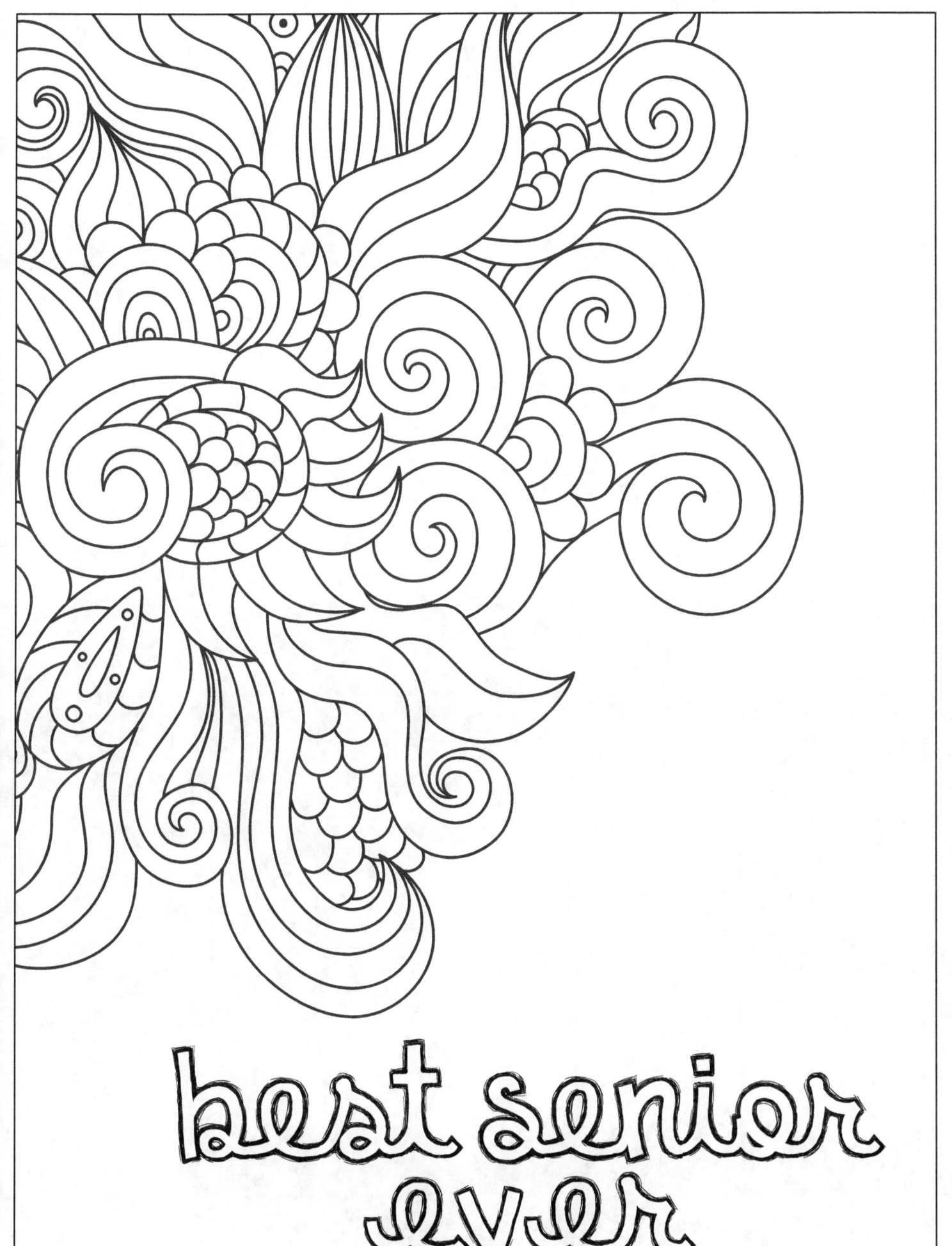

best senior ever

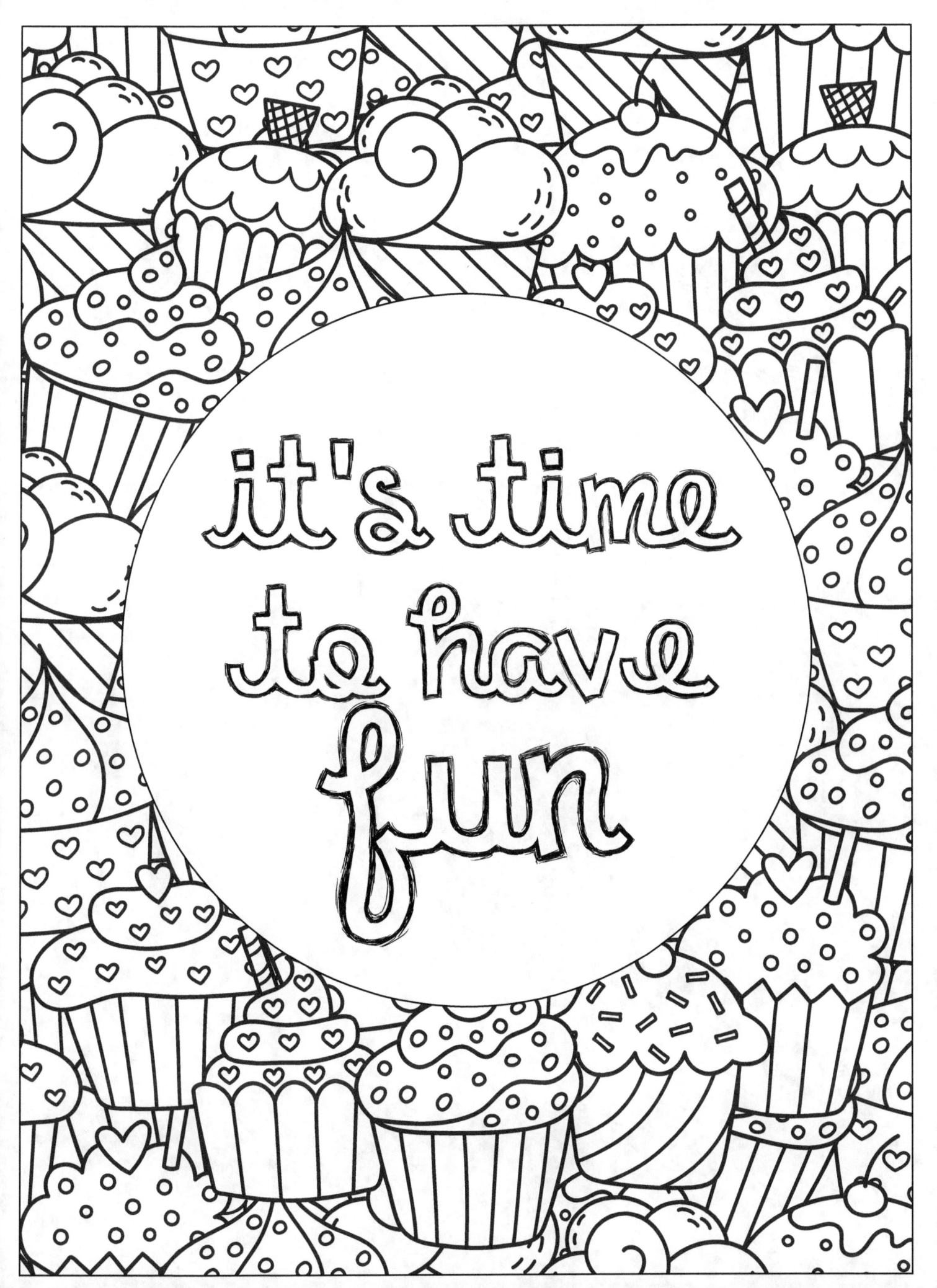

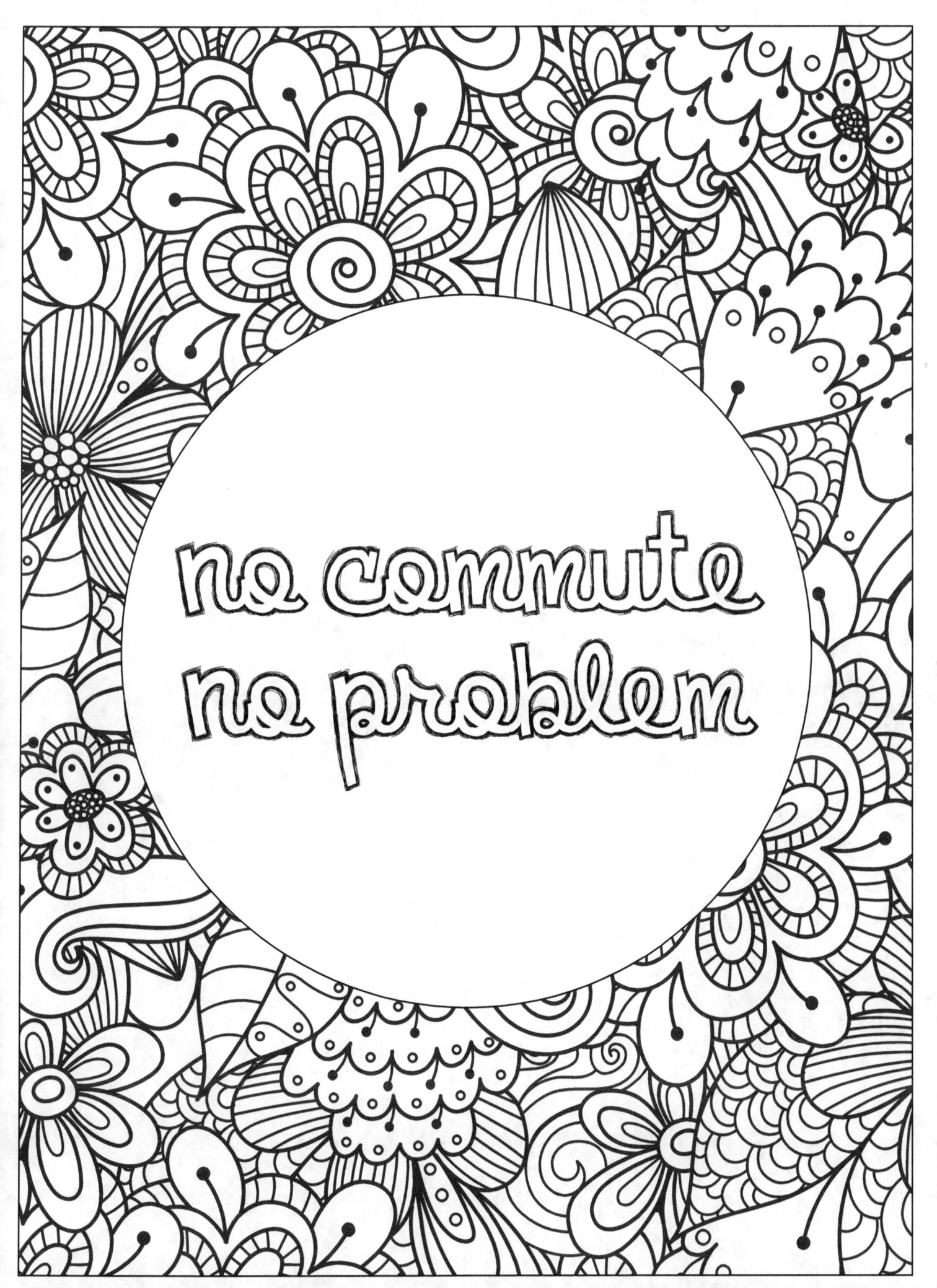

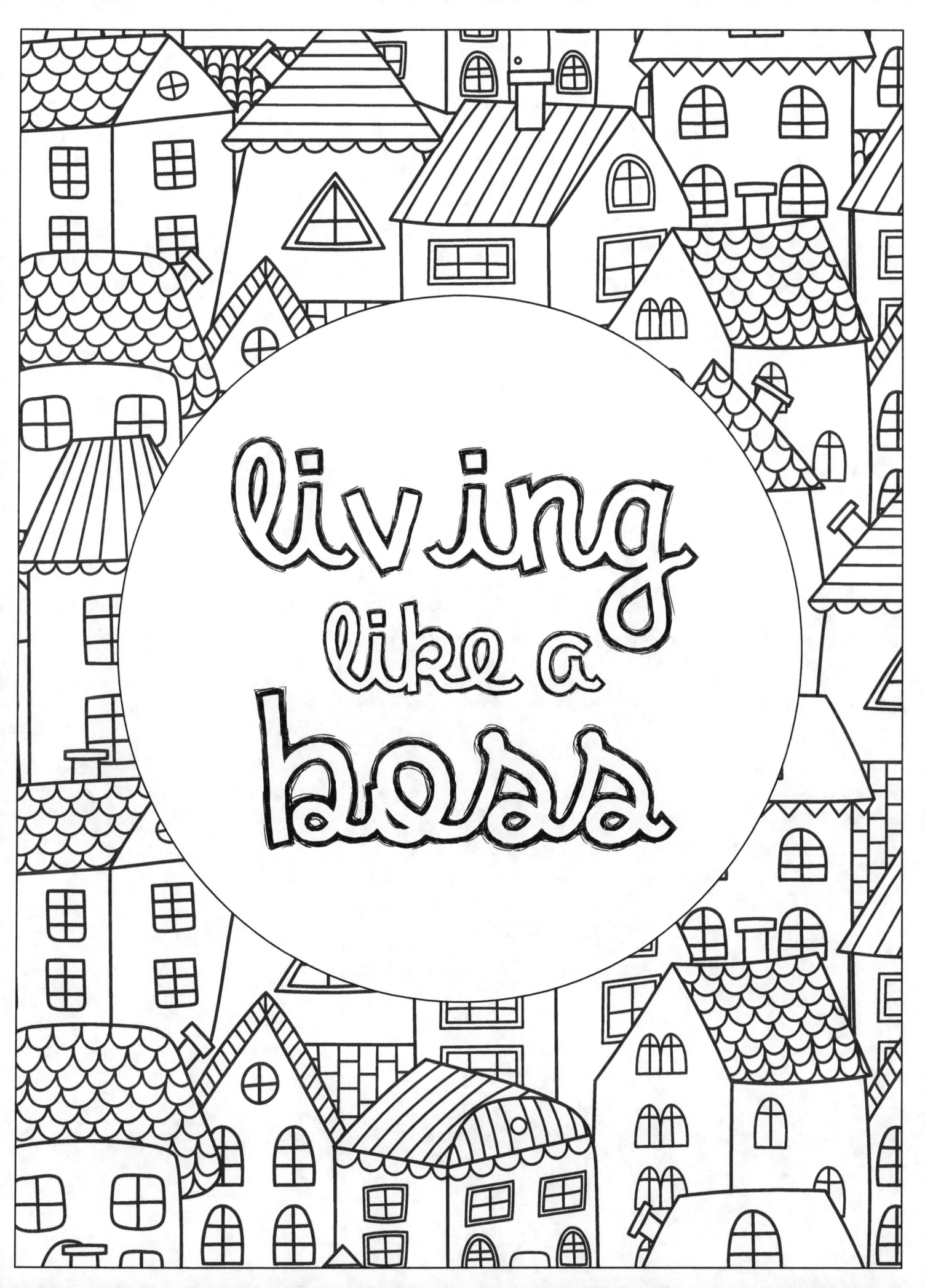

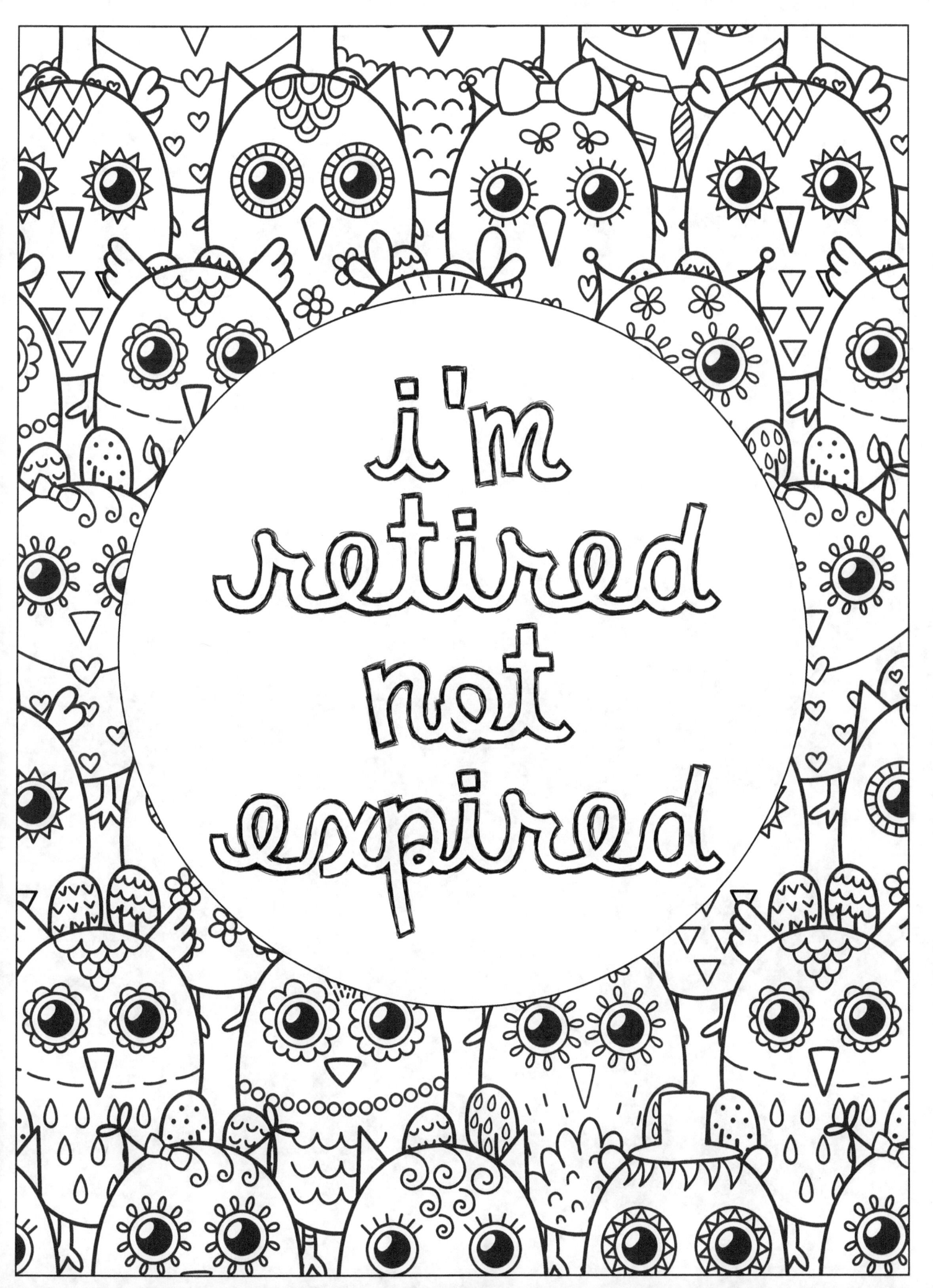

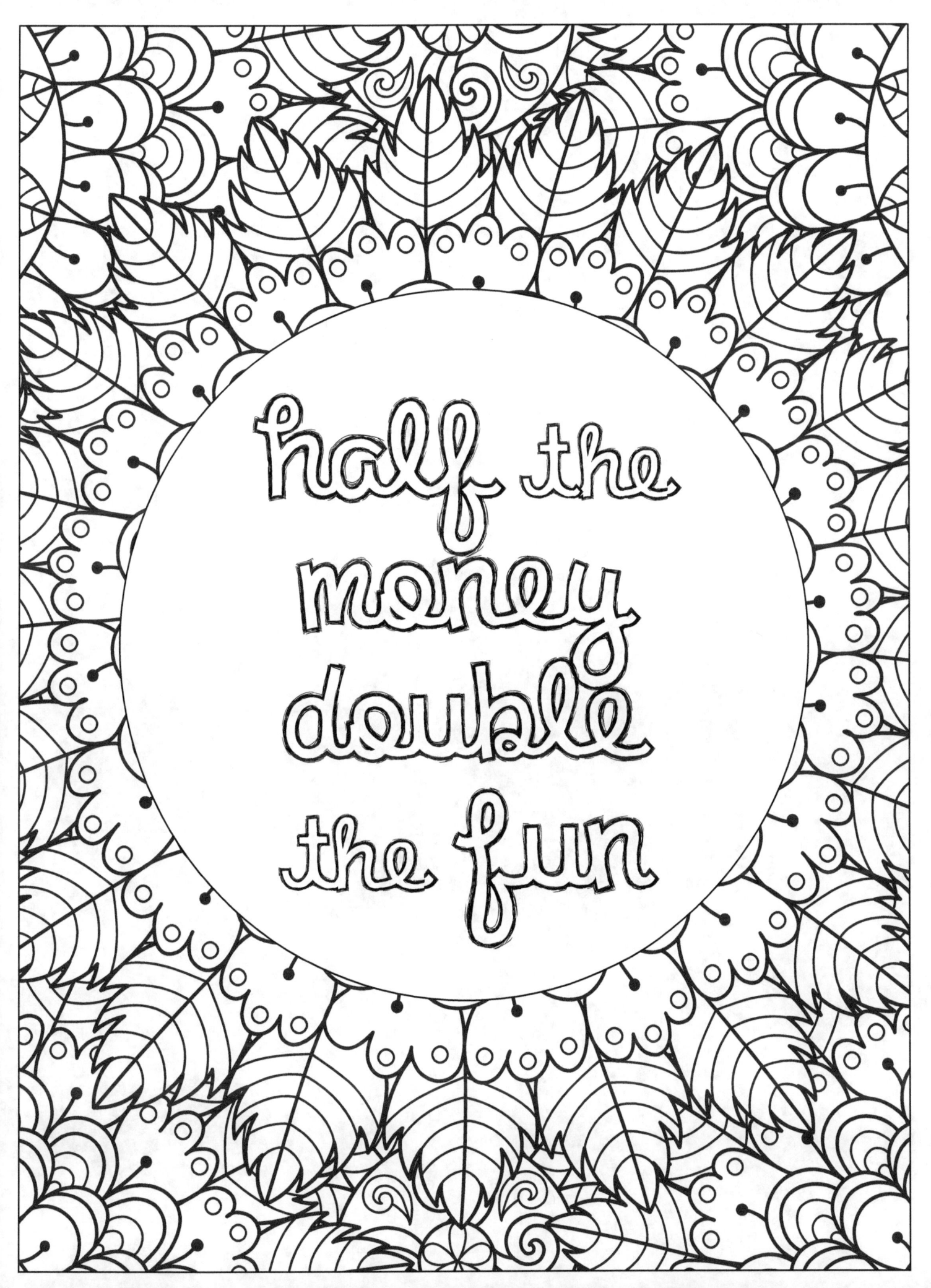

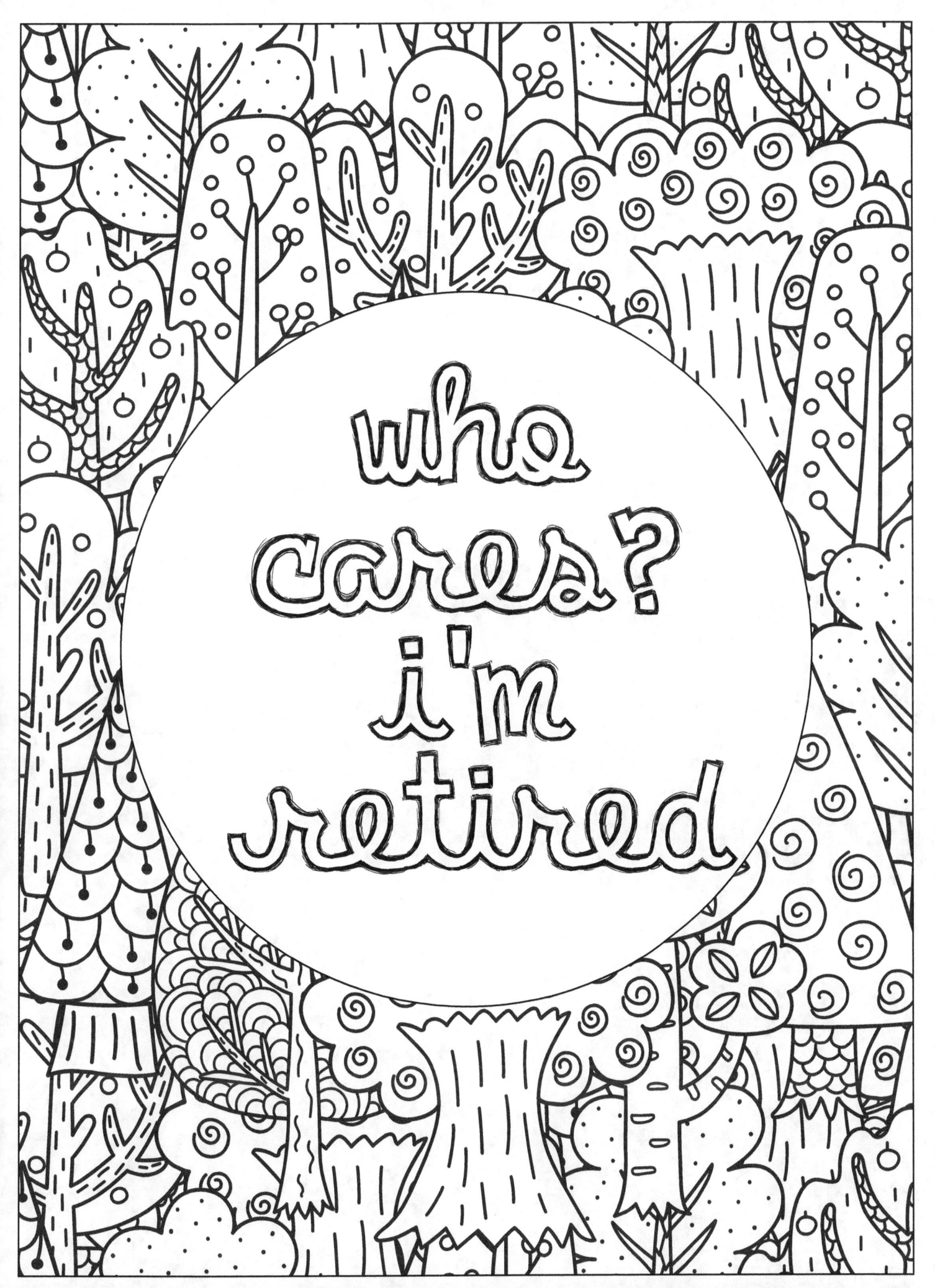

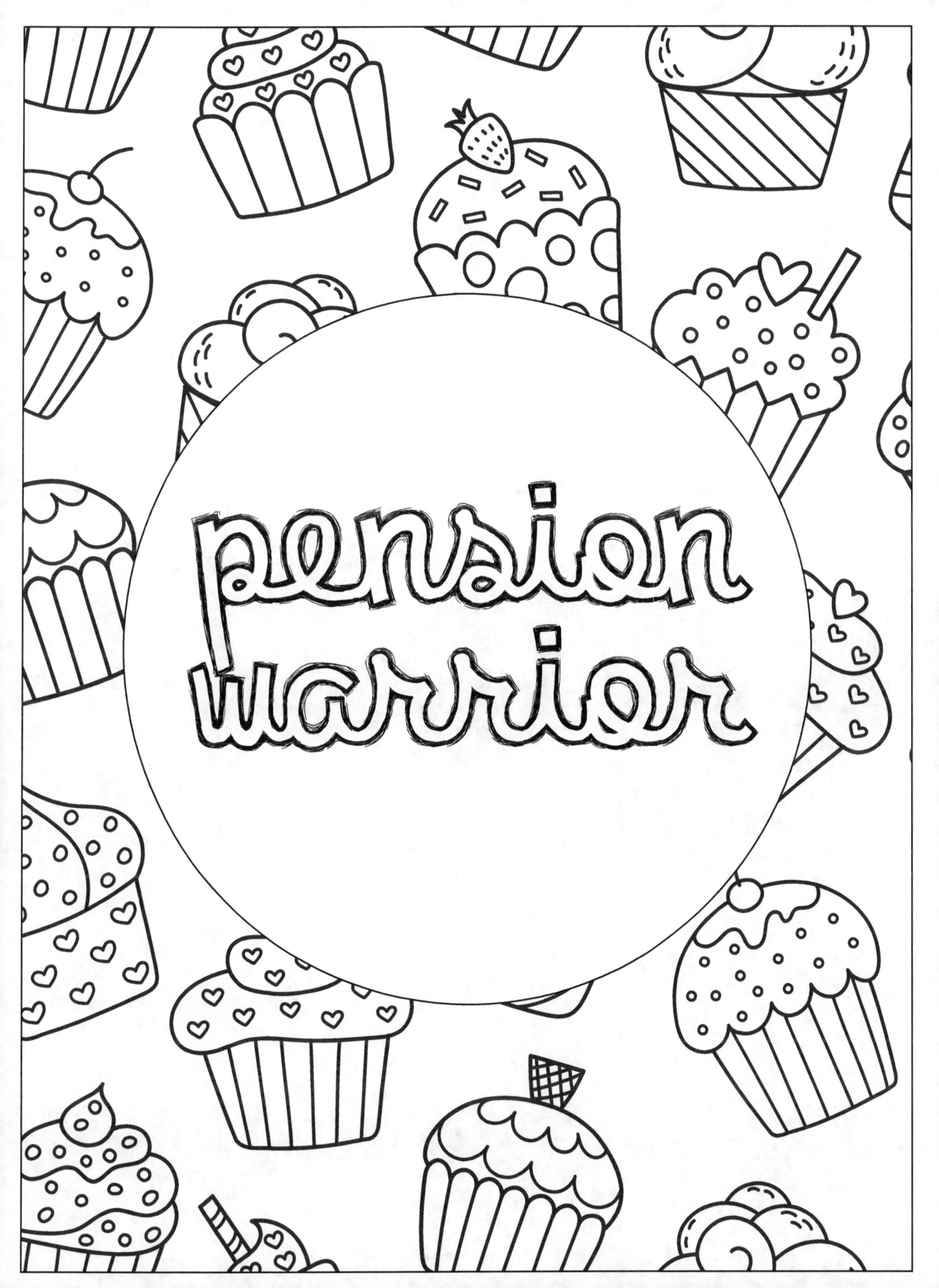

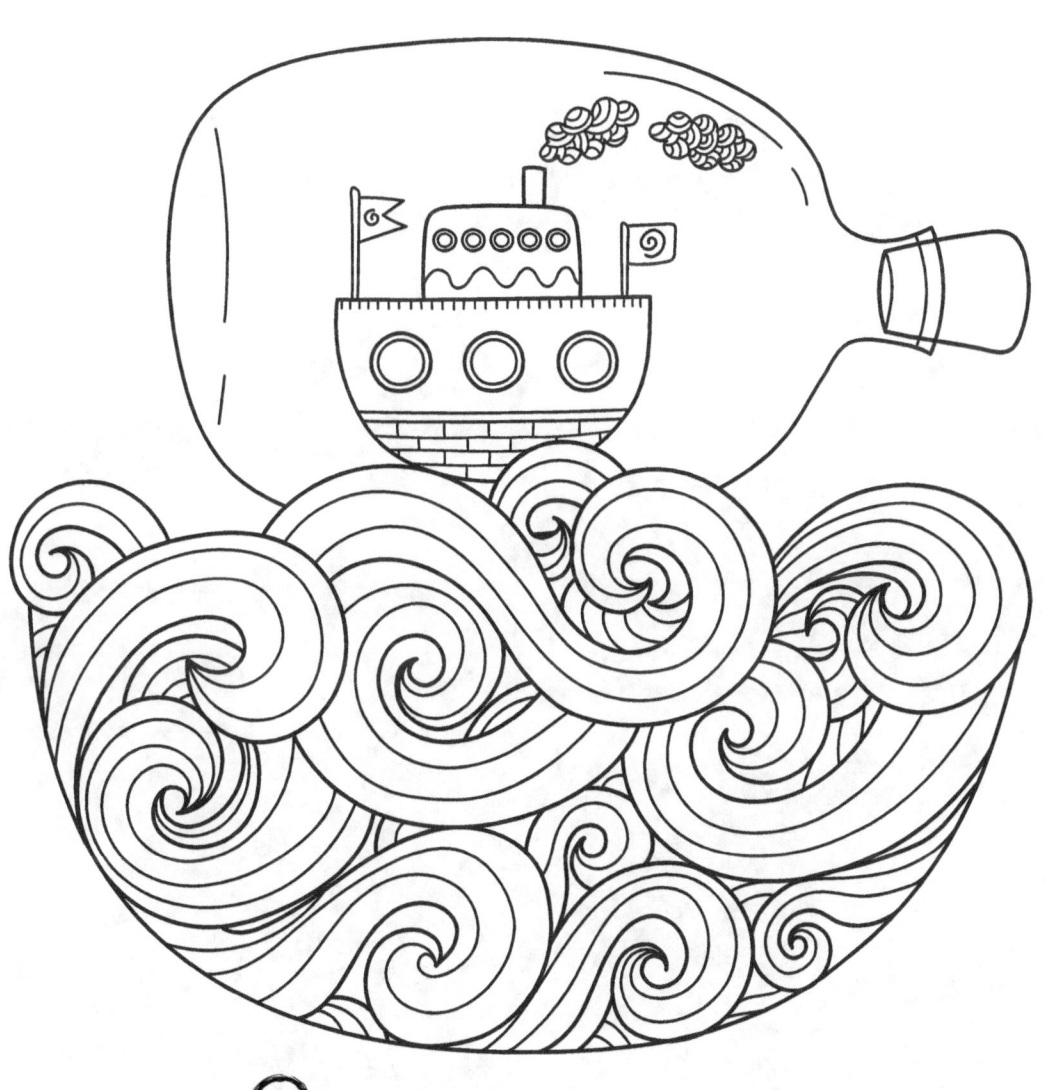

lifelong vacation

here i come

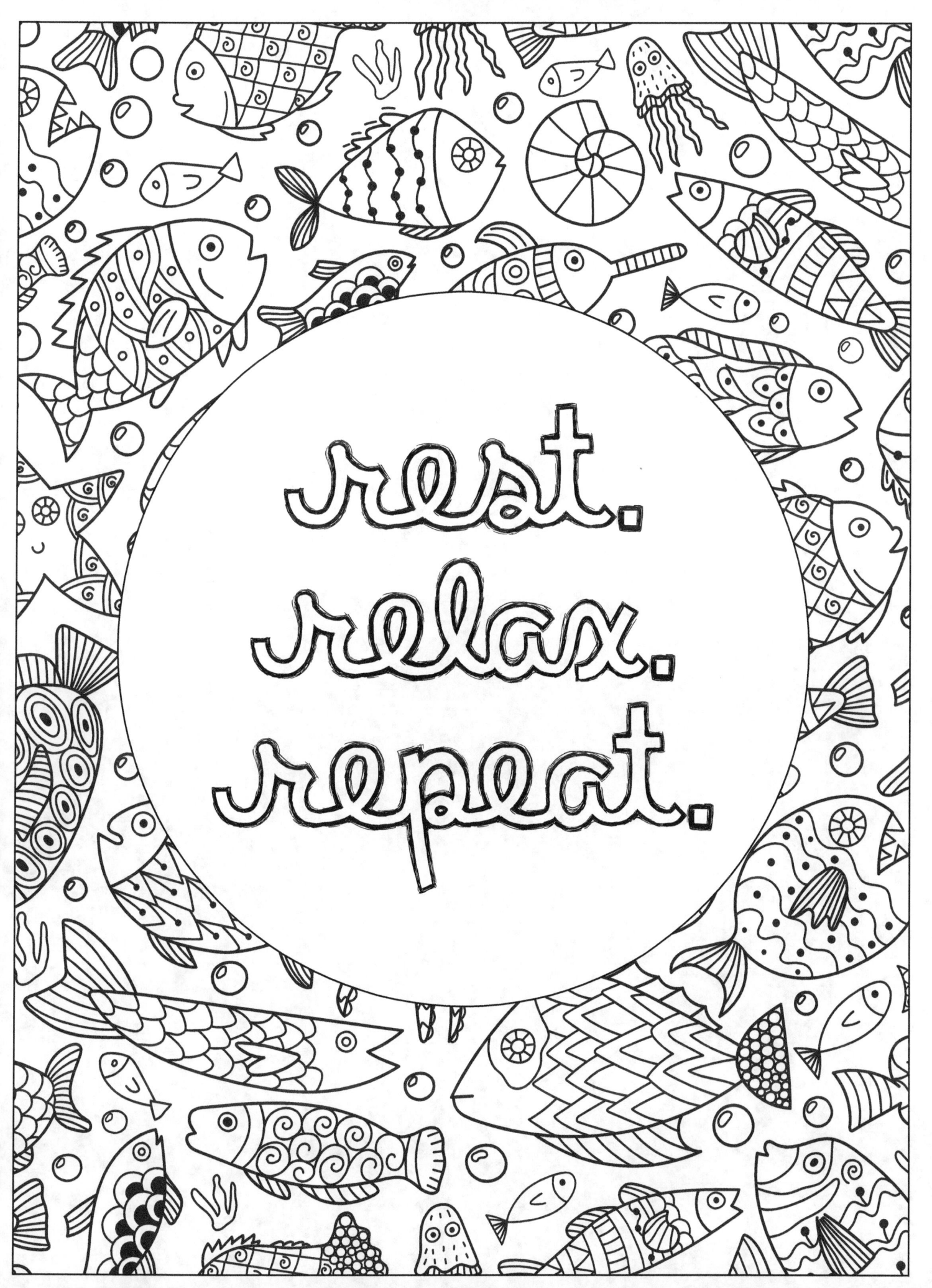

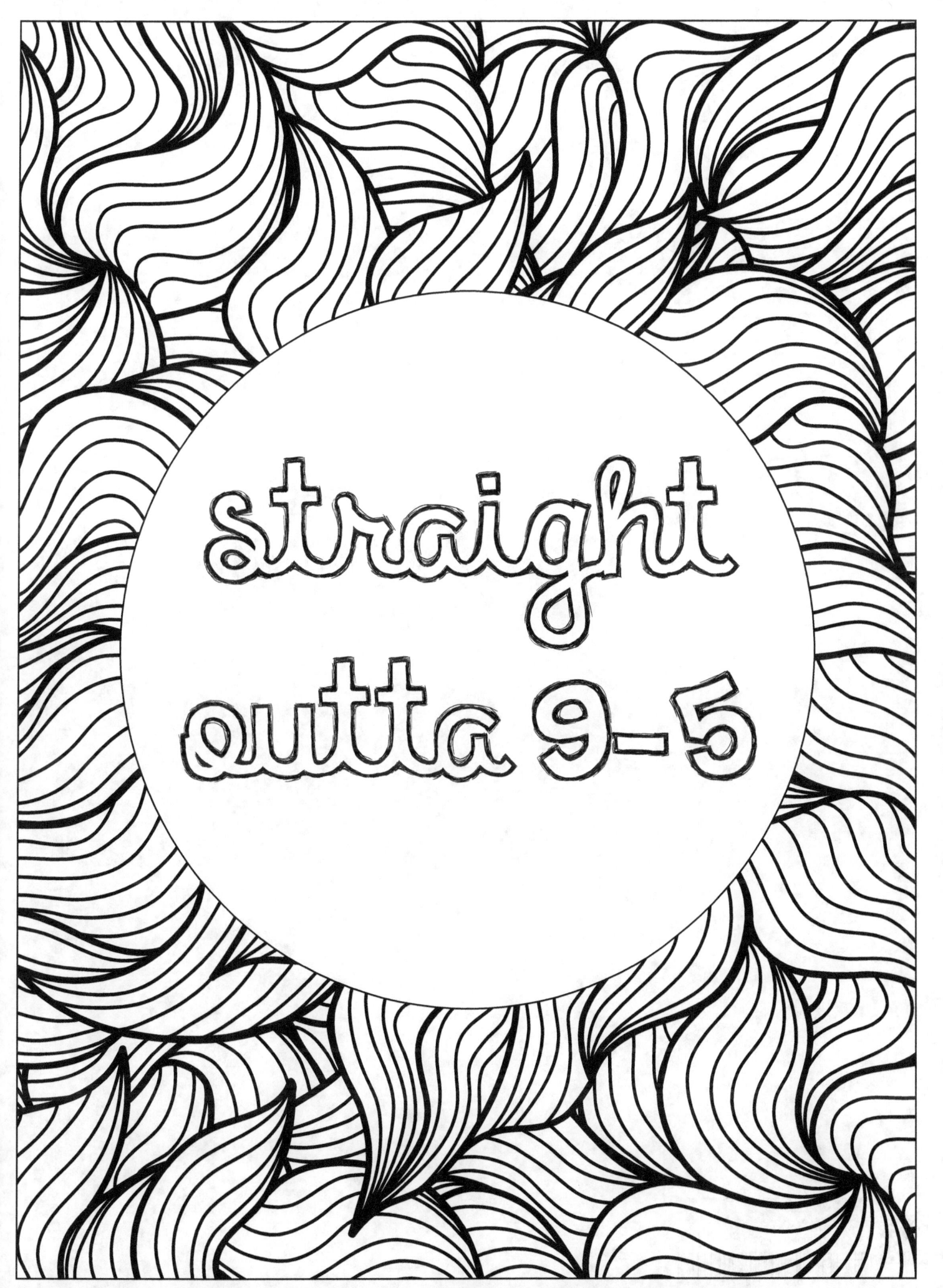